My Senses

Sight

by Nick Rebman

Focus Readers · Pioneer

www.focusreaders.com

Copyright © 2022 by Focus Readers®, Lake Elmo, MN 55042. All rights reserved. No part of this book may be reproduced or utilized in any form or by any means without written permission from the publisher.

Focus Readers is distributed by North Star Editions:
sales@northstareditions.com | 888-417-0195

Produced for Focus Readers by Red Line Editorial.

Photographs ©: Shutterstock Images, cover, 1, 4, 7, 8, 11, 12, 14 (top), 14 (bottom), 17, 18, 20

Library of Congress Cataloging-in-Publication Data
Names: Rebman, Nick, author.
Title: Sight / by Nick Rebman.
Description: Lake Elmo, MN : Focus Readers, [2022] | Series: My senses | Includes index. | Audience: Grades 2-3
Identifiers: LCCN 2021032062 (print) | LCCN 2021032063 (ebook) | ISBN 9781637390382 (hardcover) | ISBN 9781637390924 (paperback) | ISBN 9781637391464 (ebook) | ISBN 9781637391983 (pdf)
Subjects: LCSH: Vision--Juvenile literature.
Classification: LCC QP475.7 .R43 2022 (print) | LCC QP475.7 (ebook) | DDC 612.8/4--dc23
LC record available at https://lccn.loc.gov/2021032062
LC ebook record available at https://lccn.loc.gov/2021032063

Printed in the United States of America
Mankato, MN
012022

About the Author

Nick Rebman is a writer and editor who lives in Minnesota. He enjoys reading, drawing, and taking long walks with his dog. In 2021, he got his first pair of glasses.

Table of Contents

CHAPTER 1
Using Our Eyes 5

CHAPTER 2
How Seeing Works 9

CHAPTER 3
Many Colors 13

THAT'S AMAZING!
Eye Exams 16

CHAPTER 4
Keeping Eyes Safe 19

Focus on Sight • 22

Glossary • 23

To Learn More • 24

Index • 24

Chapter 1

Using Our Eyes

A rainstorm ends, and the sun comes out. Three boys step outside. They look up at the sky. They see a bright rainbow. It has many beautiful colors.

Sight is one of the five **senses**. Seeing helps us understand the world around us. We use our eyes to see. We can see many different colors.

Did You Know? Most people **blink** their eyes more than 15,000 times every day.

Chapter 2

How Seeing Works

We can see because of light. Light enters the eye. Then the light goes through a clear **lens**. After that, the light hits the back of the eye.

The back of the eye is connected to **nerves**. The nerves send messages to the **brain**. The brain gets the messages. Then the person sees.

Did You Know? The colored part of the eye is called the iris. It controls how much light goes into the eye.

Inside the Eye

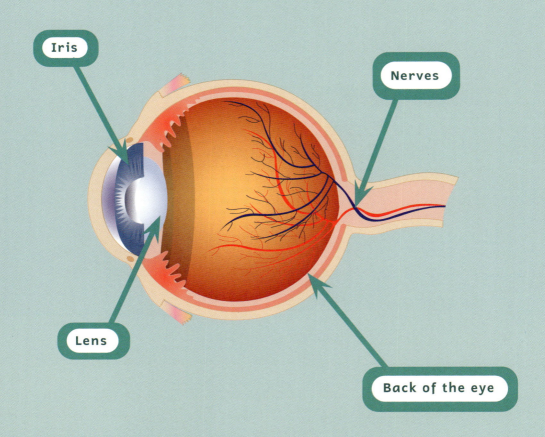

Chapter 3

Many Colors

Sight is very helpful. We can see how far away things are. We can see how big things are. We can see what color things are.

Most people can see more than one million colors. For example, a tree may have many **shades** of green. An apple may have many shades of red.

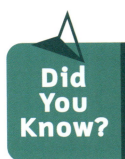

Did You Know? Some people are color-blind. They cannot tell certain colors apart.

That's Amazing!

Eye Exams

Many people's eyes do not work **perfectly**. For this reason, doctors give eye **exams**. An exam helps the doctor learn what is wrong. Then the doctor can help fix the problem. The doctor may suggest glasses. Glasses have lenses. The lenses help people see more clearly.

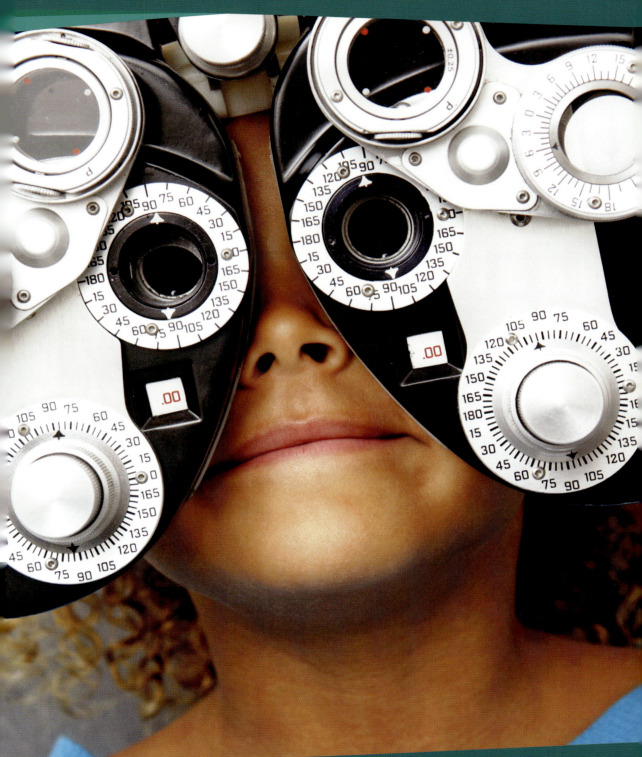

Chapter 4

Keeping Eyes Safe

Eyes can be harmed easily. So, it is important to keep them safe. On sunny days, be sure to wear sunglasses. Sunglasses stop the sun's rays from hurting your eyes.

Also, don't spend too much time looking at screens. Take a short break every 20 minutes. Take a longer break every hour.

Did You Know? Certain foods are good for your eyes. These foods include nuts, beans, and leafy green vegetables.

FOCUS ON
Sight

Write your answers on a separate piece of paper.

1. Write a sentence that explains the main idea of Chapter 2.

2. What is your favorite color? Why?

3. What sends messages to the brain?
- **A.** nerves
- **B.** lenses
- **C.** glasses

4. Why is a hat helpful on a sunny day?
- **A.** The hat can make the sun seem brighter.
- **B.** The hat can keep the sun's rays out of your eyes.
- **C.** The hat can help you see more colors.

Answer key on page 24.

Glossary

blink
To open and close the eyes quickly.

brain
The body part inside the head that helps us think.

exams
Tests that help doctors figure out what is wrong.

lens
A clear, curved surface that bends light.

nerves
Body parts that sense things and send messages to the brain.

perfectly
Without any problems or mistakes.

senses
Ways the body takes in information about the world.

shades
Colors that are similar to one another but a little bit darker or lighter.

To Learn More

BOOKS

Berne, Emma Carlson. *Let's Explore the Sense of Sight.* Minneapolis: Lerner Publications, 2020.

Hansen, Grace. *Light.* Minneapolis: Abdo Publishing, 2019.

NOTE TO EDUCATORS

Visit **www.focusreaders.com** to find lesson plans, activities, links, and other resources related to this title.

Index

B
brain, 10
C
color, 5–6, 13, 15
E
eye exams, 16

L
lens, 9, 11, 16
N
nerves, 10–11
S
sunglasses, 19

Answer Key: **1.** Answers will vary; **2.** Answers will vary; **3.** A; **4.** B